The Sky Over *Walgreens*

The Sky Over *Walgreens*

Chris Green

For Debby —
I miss your...
our RHINO days...
especially your
dining room!

Love,
[signature]

Mayapple Press, 2007

Published by   Mayapple Press
                408 N. Lincoln St.
                Bay City, MI 48708
                www.mayapplepress.com

ISBN 978-0932412-546

ACKNOWLEDGMENTS

These poems have appeared, some in different versions, in the following publications:

After Hours "New Love Crosses Busy Street"; *Columbia Poetry Review* "A Dog Named Soul," "New Year Moon Cakes"; *Court Green* "Ode to Julie Christie"; *5 AM* "A Fishing Poem," "JM," "Limbo," "All of Us"; *Five Fingers Review* "Hair Tips for Poets"; *Folio* "The Night My Grandmother Dies I Watch a Documentary About Sharks"; *Karamu* "Nursing Home Love Poem"; *MARGIE* "Thoughts of Business"; *Nimrod* "The Painting in the Jury Room," "The Physics of Ex-Girlfriends"; *North American Review* "Death at the Barnes & Noble Information Desk"; *Paterson Literary Review* "Morning Ritual"; *Poet Lore* "Poem"; *Poetry East* "Marriage: Field or Meadow?," "Common House Spider"; *RATTLE* "My Brother Buries His Dog"; *Tampa Review* "Have you seen me?," "His Closet," "Poetry Reading"; *The Cream City Review* "In the Blue Stairwell"; *The Ledge* "Ode to an Insect in Wet Paint"; *The Literary Review* "The Most Beautiful Pigeon in the World"; *The Marlboro Review* "The Sky Over Walgreens"; *The Mid-America Poetry Review* "A Woman at Starbucks Reads the Cliff Notes to *Moby-Dick*"; *Verse* "Fertility Woes, So We Go to Breed in Hawaii's Shallow Waters"

Cover art by Michelle Albandoz; author photo by Laura Friedlander. Cover and book design by Judith Kerman with text in Calisto MT and titles in Abadi Condensed MT and Brush Script Standard. Typeset by Amee Schmidt.

Contents

III.

Special Thanks

Thanks to my Bennington mentors: April Bernard, Amy Gerstler, Ethelbert Miller, and Ed Ochester. Thanks to my many poetry people in Chicago, especially Jan Bottiglieri, Larry Janowski, Richard Jones, Tony Trigilio, and David Trinidad.

For Lexa

I.

Nursing Home Love Poem

I've never told anyone this.
I lean in to give her a peck,
but before I can say, *Grandma, it's me, Chris,*
she slips me her tongue,

and I sit back and think about who I am.

I want you, she says, *I want you to kiss me.*
I miss your lips, she sighs, hot and dry with death.

I look past her body to the old family photos.

Often I am her dead children,
her long-gone mother, once even her last best dog.
Today I am her mindless memory of his mouth,
Mexican skin, the young man before he became the hard husband.

Pedro? she asks, as if I've forgotten:

Remember, we met at the harvest dance. You tipped your poor hat and
we waltzed circles in the dust, and later, behind a full strawberry truck, I
kissed you. It was the truth, before we lived in that chicken coop, before we
moved to that mining town, before I died, and I loved you.

A Fishing Poem

I know readers tense when they see a poem about fishing and
grandfathers, but we were fishing as grandfathers and grandsons do,
and this was just after his youngest daughter Gale died,
      and

          instead of a fish, he'd caught a bat skimming insects in the
          moonlight.
              It was caught not in water's mirror but the open
          mouth of night—
its furious wing beats brushed our hair, and not a scream
              but higher pitched singing touched our ears—
          in that dark, our eyes were blind black beads—
          pure listening—
and Grandpa Pete, who knew grief's long pull, one son already
          dead,
calmly drew it in—
          wings long as a baby's arms and all skin
bent around his fingers like a child's would—
              how they held each other—the picture of perfect
          love—
and as he reached past tiny teeth
              a black heart flew from his chest—
          that's how I remember it—a releasing—
a wild winging over the dark edge of suddenly something open

Morning Ritual

I'm writing a note to a man I knew. One of his two daughters just committed suicide and I'm sitting in my living room trying not to use too much of my best stationery. As if everything's fine, I ask my wife, "What do you say to a father whose daughter just shot herself?" From the shower she calls, "Keep it short!"

I write, "I'm terribly sorry. I heard about your loss and am thinking of you." Later, she comes from the bathroom nude, reads, tells me to reorder and to add fond memories of their family, which I do. "I heard about your loss and am terribly sorry. I'm thinking of you and remember you fondly."

I ask her for the last time how it sounds. She says, "Nothing you can say will make him feel any better." I remember loving that same knowing tone on our first date. I was testing to see how she felt about heaven: I remember her saying quite plainly, "Death is for the living."

Elegy with a Bee Inside It

I found it in the basement, a dead bee in a cup of nails.

It's hard to see anything in the dark,
Foxglove or plunger, tool box or hedgerow.

I like the close-up, the detail of the fur, a bumblebee's
Jagged legs and fairy wings, this one black with a band of white.
And nails as a kind of light.

I like the poignant pointlessness of it.

The bee never bothered anyone that I know of.

This is how it is, a bee seeks an exit, its eyes dark as its body.

Talking to a Dog

Emerson said all language is fossil poetry. He also said a poem is a confession of faith.
Dogs are fond of Emerson?
Woof. (A bark can be anything from a scream to hello to where did you go.)

Your favorite toy is a plastic human foot. Why?
It squeaks, and the toenails are painted a deep appetizing pink.

What mystery is this?
You are all hands and secrets, bedroom sounds and grudges.
What mystery is this?
I've listened and sniffed, I've put my head against your door, breathed the puzzle of your bones.
You might be God.
I woke you every morning so you could see the sunrise like a strong tea. Our early walks like your mother guiding you through early life.
I never forgave my mother.
Forgive her. I've pawed at your root. On his death bed, your grandfather said, Don't put things off.

People say we look alike.
There's a big difference between us. I bring my face to food; you bring food to your face.
I see this as a similarity.
Men, like dogs, know love and fear. I taste the air. Fear is salt, and its brother, Anger, is pure and clear like drinking water. Love is like flour or fresh bread, and its sister, Regret, is cinnamon. The rest tastes of flesh.

Anger?
If there is anger in me, it is squirrels. I'd like to take their trees and small funds of nuts and leave them with nothing but their precious acrobatics. I could go on.
I heard if there's nothing solid to hide behind, you can hold off a vicious dog by simply placing a blank sheet of paper in front of its face.
Yes. It's a rational fear of stationary. A world papered with possibility becomes a wall.

It's enough to make dogs question?
*No, but they dream. Like Pablo Neruda, I see things tree to tree. My
dreams are turkeys, usually turkeys. They're plucked and lined up, the
floor is slick and I bowl myself into a feast, but then there's nothing, a
burst of feathers and empty air.*

Fear?
That I wasted your life.

Regret?
I regret we never spoke before this.

Love?
I love you.
But you're dead. You starved yourself for a week and like a saint
your eyes went cloudy then clarified. I found you in the living
room. What do you have to say for yourself?
What's death?

He was gentle with machines,

never slapped or kicked
anything that could take it.
He worried over
lawn mowers, toasters, clocks,
old fishing poles,
anything without a name.
We leaked love
while he fixed the
sprinkler heads—they grew
until they sprayed full,
glowed like suns.
He doted
on knots and gnarls
of wire and line, cord
he unsnarled. Meanwhile,
his wife was
missing parts, the
cat and dog rusting.
His whole life
he never stripped a screw,
or locked up a nut.
The first time
I worked under
his hood, I cursed
as men should, insisted
on twisting too hard
while *he*
held the washers for once,
and I stabbed him,
by accident
with the screwdriver
—*Oedipus* in the driveway.

His Closet

As a boy I played house in my father's closet.
He was never home,
not in the wild checks and awful stripes of his drinking days,
lost in the smear of kissed collars Mom washed.
I searched for change in the dark pockets near his heart,
in the woolen womb of grays and blues that wore him,
cloth worked thin as skin.
I folded myself
in folds,
felt for his best suit,
the one he wore to funerals,
where, in a living tomb
I'd disappear, not wanting to go to school . . .
nothing to bear, his too soft arms for me to hit or hold,
just him there above his shoes,
hanged in Grandpa's coat,
a blackness that fit him for a time,
his father's ghost.

A Dog Named Soul

At the art fair I met a woman in a wheel chair.
She had a large dog wearing an
       orange vest that said, "Human Companion."
       She said her dog's name
and meant it. He was everything.

I hate to put my dead dog Otis in a poem;
it feels cowardly and vain, whereas he was truly brave
in a way dog-people know.

I want to call this poem, "My Dog's Life,"
but I only know his life through mine
and I hate myself as I write.

I have a cheap routine I could do
about how his death
reminds me of the brother I neglect.
I could weave in a whole shtick about absolute innocence.
I could even describe the woman's weakness.
I could say Otis is everything I've never done.

He was just a dog (and sometimes I was mean).

Old friend, I loved you, and I'm sorry.

My Brother Buries His Dog

He moves furniture for a living, oversized bureaus and beds for the rich. He is big now and dumb with love that animals sense—cats, dogs, squirrels, birds, his pygmy turtles and rabbits, tree frogs—they all take him in, nuzzle his childhood scars, forgive his bad jobs and girlfriends. The middle child who grew up telling us all to fuck off—now a grown man—calls me crying, *Why my puppy?* (His Great Dane is dead.) He sobs, and I remember how we beat him—Mom, Dad, nuns, coaches, teachers—I know I did. And like animals before a storm, he has premonitions—this time a dream of me crying over Nina's corpse. He says, *I want you to think about that.* He says it because I'm the godless eldest son who knows everything. So we carry his huge dead dog from the vet to his truck to his backyard. He digs a hole all day then lays her black body in the dark. Weeping, he seals her in with a last block of sod, and between the kiddy pool and the garage we embrace. He whispers, *I love you.* And in that moment I knew what animals know.

Best Friend

Jimmy John Wiscom was, before
he burned down his parents' fence and my mother
declared him off limits.
But before, when I was free to meet him
in the abandoned lot at the end of our street,
we captured grasshoppers.
I would catch the things,
sharp feet
testing and tickling the walls of my palms,
their buzzing and shrieking like a small machine.
What Jimmy John did next
reminds me that nothing and no one is safe.
I would hand him the narrow body—
its large eyes surprised
(I remember how they spit
in my hand, a weak but significant gesture).
Jimmy John would hold it
down by the abdomen with his thumb,
often too hard,
and the green blood would bleed from the end.
And then, because this was play,
he would methodically pull off each of its legs
(loves me, loves me not, loves me).
Then he pulled off each wing.
I never knew they had wings until I saw them taken.
A lonely torso was left
sideways on the sidewalk stripped
of everything but its head.
And because that was not enough,
my once best friend would finish
by popping it into his mouth
and swallow hard
so I could see his Adam's apple up and down.
He would smile and open big.
There was nothing but the hollow
of his throat
and his clean, menacing teeth.

The Seal

Seagulls bright like sails,
girls
with golden hair and skin,
the sweet sight of bodies in the sun
—glistening, at play, in love—
sea calm, air warm, water clear and cool,

and not far down the beach, a seal
chained to a stake as if punished.

It bore a heavy corroded collar
that cut a raw ring
of dried blood and blubber, the flesh
a gore of gull bites—
the eyes and pretty pointed nose
pecked deep, bright red openings.
The flippers hung
oversized, lifeless,
a clown's useless hands and shoes.
Nude, but for its blood,
the seal alone
among the terrible gulls, a thousand flies.

Weekend-ers at joy and laughter,
we gathered to see, shivered, then broke apart.
No one cried out.

I must have asked why. Who could know?

This was a happy day.
We'd driven west to the edge of land.
Dad guilty but smiling
brought his briefcase to the beach.
Mom collecting and cleaning shells to show him
hoping for a wave of recognition, emotion.
There's a photo, off-center, more sea than
family.

Have you seen me?

Lost between bills and birthday cards
a plea to the resident at this address.

Age-progressed, lost for years,
the smiling paper face of a boy transformed:

How appealing to his parents,
rendered safely old, hair combed, wearing a sweater.

How noble, this slip of hope,
like putting an old lamp out on the porch for the poor.

I think about who is taken—
that lost boys are looked for, but not as men.

What I Can Tell Ted Kooser and No One Else

Grandma Zella in her small tar-papered house
crocheted miniature sombreros for my mom's mini-bottles
of scotch. The radio cried its country song, and there was a bar
across the street. In the yard, a large lilac bush grows larger
in my memory, its purple and blue blooms a violent beauty;
and, tied to its base, one in a series of tall brown hunting dogs
all named Lucky, each eventually poisoned by someone
who'd crushed glass in meat. There was the hardness
of Grandpa Pete. Three of her children died while
she was alive. And there propped on her T.V. next to a
blood red bull with gold horns from Mexico, was the painting
on driftwood I did for her of green mountains with snowy tops.

The Night My Grandmother Dies I Watch a Documentary About Sharks

Surrounded by bull sharks
and standing in three feet of water
in which he'd dropped fish heads
and lamb parts, Shark Gordon's
heart rate is seventy-four. He says
sharks sense fear through changes
in our heart: the sharks
quicken and circle, then disappear
as a long shadow approaches.
He slaps a limp fish at the water
and says he can't resist feeding
this beauty himself—a great white
rises, all jaw, a gaping submarine
ringed with teeth. And in that wide
unhinged moment, I see inside
the great room that is the shark—
the porpoise parts, a blue penguin,
a rough kitchen towel,
a small spaniel, the whole of Idaho,
her brand of hand cream, the power
of pain, a swirl of white hair.
When the shark finally recedes,
waves darken, and after
a silence, Shark Gordon's voice,
"This is why I wake up every morning."
And then it's herself and myself
and the whole cradling sea.

In the religion of horses,

trail rides are nose-to-rear funeral marches, horse heads asking
why why each bob and step, everything they say a high short cry.
Let us consider what it is to have a horse named Pedro, my grand-
father's name. Not a horse done up in ribbons, but a horse like
my grandfather with no religion. He runs trying to shake his rider
because he knows things he cannot say.

II.

Ars Poetica

for Richard Jones

I get lonely and think of my dog.
He was the most basic of souls,
a black Lab with a stiff-legged walk.
Part grandfather, part toddler,
a mongrel like everyone, he loved
to hump too much when he was young.
He was right about everything—
his kindness, his stubbornness.
From the window above my desk,
I'd see him in the yard, a black spot
against a blank page of snow.
Nose down, reading carefully,
he would stop and paw,
his snout in a kind of kissing,
and he would begin digging
for spring. Like poetry,
he understood more
by not understanding. I want to
die without knowing I'm dying,
to love the ground and dig
for sweet bones, to lie in doorways
at night, and in the morning
take in the sunlight.

Elegy for the Horse Himself

I can't write as Larry Levis so I'll say he was my favorite horse.
He was so beautiful we called him Beauty, and people would
        stop by
Our pasture and ask if they could buy him. He was a mix of
        grey and blue,

Like stratus clouds and summer sky.

A quarter-horse, he ran fast but not far. Beauty was impossible
        to ride—
At full gallop he was wind parting long grass, a song to himself,
        a hymn

To some lost west.

A drawing of him hangs in my parents' basement: an "A+"
        with a note,
"The tones of this horse!" The shading and shape I learned
        from him:

You don't want a sorrowful horse, but stoic.

I try to capture the horse himself—the face, its fine veining;
        a nostril resembles
A teardrop; the torso a cylinder of light.

Anna Akhmatova

She once compared Boris Pasternak to the eye of a horse, he "peers, looks, sees, identifies, / and instantly like molten diamonds / puddles shine, ice grieves and liquefies." She too sees in elegies. Poet as witness and funeral horse tiptoeing through waist-high snow. It was an old Petersburg road through her ruined marriage and rotting government. There were no tears; she was no exile; she faced the land and spoke straight of everything plundered, betrayed, sold. There is something shining in her grief. She sees history as brutal and coarse; her words are lovely but dead-cold. Through the wind, trees, and snow, she sees the graveyard and is home.

Matthews Music

The words he uses most are *fire, tongue, light, love, dog,* and *beer.*
"And a beer for our reticence, / the true tongue, the one song, the
fire made of air." In "Beer after Tennis, 22 August 1972," he
drives home to feed his dog as the earth turns and the sun seems
to fall. He produced a new book every three years, his last, *After All,*
just days before his death. He wrote to instruct but also comfort,
"It's OK, we're only dying." His theme: cherish what you lose—
each poem a short life lived wisely, and always moving. Of John
Coltrane, he said, "Hearing him dead, I feel it in my feet." Of
Mingus, "He's all the light there is." Jazzmen and dogs (friends
that all die young). And like jazz, and like life, he spoke the truth,
"fire burns wherever it goes." But he writes in loving tones, each poem
a letter to a friend, and he ends, "yrs, burning outward, Bill"

Hair Tips for Poets:

1.
Look at Frost: "The clouds were low and hairy in the skies,
Like locks blown forward in the gleam of eyes."
2.
Remember, hair is a miracle, like metaphor.
At your desk, rake your fingers through its sea.
3.
A bad perm spondees, a *heartbreak* or *nightmare*
(this gives your poem that harsh, artificial look).
4.
If the hairline's receding, call it snow-melt,
Cut what you must.
5.
At times, the poem must lift:
Dry your hair upside down—mother did.
6.
Chop one lemon   2-cups water   spritz:
There's poetry in home-made hair spray.
7.
Hair should never be surprising.
Inevitably, hair should be silent.
8.
Hair should lie naturally like snow.
Hair worn long should not be prose.
9.
Massage the scalp with ice water.
Each strand an exquisite lament.
10.
Comb with emotion.
Where there's death, there are hats.

New Year Moon Cakes

I crack the heart-shaped cookie,
but no fortune. No slip filled with portent,
nothing even to resent, and I laugh self-consciously thinking
this is bad, this nothing. I call the waiter, "Nothing?"

The waiter says his boss buys the cookies in bulk
from Golden Dragon Incorporated. My mind journeys
and I inspect not the vats of bleached malted
barley flour, not the tubs of potassium bromate and Yellow #6,

but the simple table where the Dragon's wise men sit
at tiny typewriters. I ask the wisest what *nothing* means.
He types the word *nothing* and hands it to me.
Everything we eat has a message, every watermelon seed

a word; presliced cheese reveals corporate secrets;
lettuce says something about our flesh, how delicate;
bananas promise ultimate truth.
I eat the cookie, lonely for its fortune. I taste nothing.

My placemat says fortune cookies formed the basis of the Ming
dynasty. They were first known as New Year Moon Cakes
made from Lotus Nut Paste—the Mongols occupied China
for centuries but had no taste for the paste, so the Chinese

fed the treat to their own and in it slipped the date of the uprising.
Later, in America, Chinese '49ers built the great railways
and made biscuits with wishes inside that did not say,
"You will be buried beneath the tracks you laid."

A new round of cookies is brought to our table:
Alas! The onion you are eating is someone else's water lily.
A modest man never talks to himself.
Nothing is not yet lost.

Limbo

In the map of Dante's hell, he neglects to note
the circle for listening to a lecture on Dante's hell.
The speaker keeps speaking,

something something something
about romantic poetry and the bitch of meaning.
The woman next to me yawns, slips off her shoes,

each foot the nude torso of a sculpted perfect form,
each arch the entrance to an Italian church.
A quick religion gazing on these soles—

her one foot mounts the other
tapping terza rima, the toes' tiny branchings,
and the nails glossed and eternal, painted

a whorish red. O tolerance, tolerance of tolerance,
she is the pregnant wife of a friend: a "language poet"
who lives in a heaven of his own baloney.

I once helped him move his futon from one poor apartment
to the next. On the way, the bed flew from the back
of my truck, landed on the freeway perfectly made.

It was the first time he ever smiled without being drunk or
borrowing money, and I wait for the poem where his Beatrice
conceives on a lonely freeway of endless wordplay.

The Writing Poem

(Response to **Writing: The Story of Alphabets and Scripts** *by Georges Jean)*

In rooms marked MEN,
the etched and embellished caves of our age, no ancient buffaloes
        and antelope
but indiscreet beavers, the ubiquitous phallus—

pictographs no less primitive than the first from the 4th
        millenium B.C.:
head of an ox to indicate "ox"; a pubic triangle with a mark for the vulva
representing "woman," "mountains" added the idea of a foreign woman,
that is, one who had come from the other side of the mountains—
meaning "female slave."

Seduction by inscription: monks wrote on vellum, skin,
but were copyists not composers. The dark urge to ink the pen—
the fearful calligraphy of God's finger—the art where each stroke
        is a sailor arriving at port.

Placed under the sign of the goddess Io, all letters of the alphabet are born.
I and O allow the meeting of the straight line and the circle,
symbolize the two organs of generation.

Outside my room, I account for children chasing children in the
        schoolyard.
A child's sprint is cursive angling imperfect long loose bodied *y*'s,
        moving *o*'s.

Inside my room, I print *A* and see a man in full stride, the crossbar
        covering his genitals:
man's admission to write.

Thoughts of Business

> *the black chairs howl endlessly*
> *— Pablo Neruda*

I am a small typist,
I have pale geraniums and no parking space, I have short hair and
so many things I must
      forget, I reconcile three subsidiary reports to the monthly
summary report to ensure the summary report includes the
amounts in the three subsidiary reports.

I fit into my desk as bone into flesh,
I sing of clean bathrooms and no moon, there is money and there
is more money, I sing
      the modern warehouse stacked with forgetting, Oh my
heart! O clocks, O my cubicled fluorescence and general absence
of hope, O CEO, O Mercedes S Class, O sickness, O work.

      O Pablo, my cursor swerves like swallows and all that I see
      is wall.
On lunch breaks, I translate your messages—they are moist with
      sea foam.

O my spiny pencils, O paper in your business white—I sing of
America spread out like a
      spread sheet—
What a terrible employee Walt Whitman would be—open-eyed,
refusing teamwork.
      On his first quicksand day, a boundless memo—

To: Menacing Manager
From: A Simple Separate Person
Date: Ever Continued
Re: Of Life Immense

You whirl me.
You ask, What singest thou?
You, O tan-faced VP of Operations,
You came, taciturn, with nothing to give—we but look'd on each

other,
When lo! I saw in you ascending power and I fill myself with the immensity of your
           wave.
You ask, Knowest thou the fortune of your fortune?
I answer simply, fortune varies, workers waiver, and my judgment ever-deferred.

Let the consultants descend from the stands where they are forever charging—let an
           idiot or insane person audit the auditors.
To his work without flinching the accountant comes. Death does not alarm him.
Thou client throbbest life and pride and love the same as we.

Therefore let us die and live expecting.
O perpetual transfers and promotions, O IRS—I hear you whispering there—
           O starry stock trades—O grasping—O graves,
I am but an edit, an editor, a man, I but advance a moment only to wheel and hurry
           back.

And so to you, Corporate, body of my body, I leave myself to your bitter hug,
           yet it is idle to try to define me.
I recline by the jamb of my exquisite nonexistent door.

A Woman at Starbucks Reads the Cliff Notes to *Moby-Dick*

Where to go to read your Cliff Notes? A place where Ahab and Starbuck might meet to exchange very different stories of home.

Ahab talks sadly about his wearying quest and orders one last grande white chocolate mocha caffe Americano no foam latte.

He says to the cashier, *Come and see if ye can serve me! Serve me? Ye cannot serve me, else ye serve yourself! Man has ye there. Serve me?* Ahab occasionally gets lost in language, repeating a phrase until it becomes almost meaningless, merely a sound. His speech thus becomes a kind of poetry, a music equivalent to a stir-stick.

Starbuck watches Ahab pile and pile sugar in his cup until the sum is a general white hump; Ahab continues to pile sugar in a general rage until instead of drinking he's eating a dense cake. With malice, Ahab jabs and jabs.

In despair, Starbuck wants to escape to the bathroom but can't because the key attached to the long plastic spoon is being used.

Death at the Barnes & Noble Information Desk

I need to pee and ask the simplest of questions, when
a garish espresso-sipping-super-mom-in-a-black-velvet-jogging-suit
        steps in front of me.
"Death and Dying?"

Her question should have cracked the store from
coffee bar to bargain bin,
but the clerk is calm.
"Are you looking for a particular title?"

"No, I'm just cruising."
I turn to find the goddamn bathroom for myself when
it hits me, the nature of death,
not a toads-falling-from-the-sky-end-of-the-world mystery, but

a mundane you're-left-alone-with-no one-to-tell-you-where-to-go.
Leading the way, the clerk says what every oracle
has ever said when confronted with death,
"Let me suggest Spirituality."

Together they cross the wide green carpet,
past Health & Diseases, New Releases, Mystery, Poetry,
Regional Cookbooks, Relationships, Role Playing, Romance, Self-
        Improvement.

The Painting in the Jury Room

Near a snowy cottage, two woolen children on an icy pond look suspiciously at a duck. They take offense at the glow of justice in the duck's teal breast. The duck states he will not vacate the painting, what is watery is his property, and that this winter scene has caused his family to flee. The painter claims the sky is innocent but truly magnificent, that indeed the heavens are his true subject, that he can't recall what he was doing that day, but certainly he was not provoking the snow. The prosecutor asks, "Sir, why are the young always portrayed as young? What of their elderly selves?" The artist says winter is shiny and that he cannot be convicted for shining, that low-level trial attorneys are all alike in being low, and that if he were to paint this farce of a trial he would place a swan next to a broken bucket next to a disused well before a brilliant sunset. At this, the artist's eyes sparkle, and the prosecutor becomes cheerful saying, "So, you do sparkle!" The artist breaks down and confesses how he loves to stroke the moon and peaked roofs with cold blues and freeze the movement of dresses and petticoats and the stockings of maidens.

All of Us

I think of Raymond Carver sitting in his kitchen where he eats
the brook trout he always dreamed of. From my room, I wish
he were here to see the geese fly over Chicago to Lake Michigan,
their irregular V and broad wings, a traveling wind . . . the rushing
sound itself like a great body of water, a river. To read his poems
and stories is to suddenly see the ordinary, and him, an agreeable
companion. He knew what he wrote could break down like a mar-
riage. He took large risks in his writing and his life and so failed
and succeeded largely. He liked to repeat things: *But I don't under-
stand, and I don't understand*—this was often about death coming
on, or how he saw animals as mysterious as us. He was curious.
He knew every detail, every word, but knew none of it made sense.
Yet he nods in gratitude, even in death. He was fond of fishing and
describing: he wrote to not feel dead, and he fished to be outside,
to look into water and be silent.

Poetry Reading

I cannot forget the old man at the workshop,
embarrassed, humble,
a realtor working years for himself,
never studied, not in public.

He begged our pardon in advance for any
stumbles, and began to read "The Heart Rides a Handsome Horse"
with emotion . . . his voice stepping in and out
when the poet-in-residence cut him short:

You'll have trouble finding a journal for this.
The sing-song sound and images are child-like.
And everyone, preserve yourselves from the sentimental,
feel things profoundly, but with reticence.

I cannot forget the part about an injured eagle flying,
the way he ended quietly by saying,
it was about his brother
dying

A Late Ironic Whitman of Our Industrial Heartland*

In Philip Levine, the black and white of real life, its elemental unforgiving self. And, in the clarity of his light, I see my grandfather waiting in work gloves and a worn windbreaker. Thick in the middle and thin in the limbs, he worked constantly to keep his family alive. I see the largeness of his hands worn and rough like hooves, used daily, naturally, from a family of hands strong as wire that disappear into work. I see the torque and take of the everyday. I see Levine, his "greasejobs," the seeds he turned to poetry and the easier machine of teaching, yet his poems still sing of memory's violence and tenderness. Reading him, I see my father as a young man working his way through school, shoveling dried cows' blood into box cars for fish food.

*Edward Hirsch, describing Philip Levine.

Ode for Kenneth Koch

This sounds like you: "I was brought up in Cincinnati, Ohio.
My parents were very nice. The first time I wrote a poem,
my mother gave me a big kiss and said,
    'I love you.'"
You are happy about poetry.
I think of you thinking of Keats who cultivated
    a feeling
of deliberate happiness, a state in which he could write poetry
best. You say things like, "It's a lot of fun to write in short lines."
Your illuminations have a joyful ease. But you're not easy.
You preach that we should
    not be timid.
You read Milton and Stevens to kids, you say poetry doesn't have
to make sense in the
    usual way,
you escaped Cincinnati, you educate the imagination,
you collaborate with painters,
you drop names but not to be fancy, just clear:
poets have friends, and some friends are Frank O'Hara and
John Ashbery
who both made you a little crazy, but not in the
    usual way.

JM

(written after re-reading James Merrill)

I'm interested in how many of your poems begin
at a resort hotel and end with the fact of love. I MODELED
MY POEMS AFTER BOB HOPE & BING CROSBY MOVIES—
TRAVEL MUSICALS WITH BELLY-LAUGHS
AND NICE ROOMS.
THE PLACE I'M STAYING NOW IS LOUSY WITH POETS
AND ZILLIONAIRES.
I JUST SPOKE TO A WOMAN WHO ONCE WENT
ON A SAFARI OF SORTS AND THINKS AFRICA
HAS TOO MANY ELEPHANTS.   TOM ELIOT HANDED
HER A CAT
AND TOLD HER ART CURES AFFLUENCE. WHICH IS TRUE,
NO ONE'S TOO RICH TO SURVIVE THE SUNLIGHT.
LIFE IS A DREAM WORTH SAYING, A REAL PLACE OF
WINGS AND SHOULDER BLADES,
PETS AND GUSTS OF FINE PERFUME, ORANGE
TREES, MAIDS WAFTING SUITCASES, GREEN ISLANDS
BUT ALSO BLEAK SNOW
AND THE COLD WAY WAITING. You seem just a touch
away from life.
THE MORE LIVING, THE LESS TRUTH.
Old line? Quoting yourself, even in your realm?
THE LEGEND OF NARCISSUS IS TRUE. HE KEEPS DYING,
FALLING INTO HIMSELF IN HIS BATHROOM. HIS MIRROR
TOO TIMELESS, TOO HIM. You once said,
"Nothing lasts and nothing ends."
IS THAT A QUESTION? WELL, I'M DEAD.
FROM HERE WE LEARN WHAT WE ALREADY KNOW.
WHEN YOU FEEL YOURSELF LEAVING, THE RIDDLE AT
LIFE'S CENTER BECOMES SOMETHING AS SIMPLE AS
THIS LOVELY TERRACE,
SOMETHING PRESUMPTIVE OF STARS. Then, death.
I'VE FORGOTTEN. LOOK, IT'S NICE TO DRINK TEA.
AND WE COULD EACH USE A PLACE BY THE WATER,
SOME TIME UNDER AN EXPENSIVE SUN.
This evening I'm considering cuts and changes . . .

my need to be heavy but light. Might you arbitrate?
YOU'D BEST ASK MS. BISHOP ABOUT THAT.
SHE KNOWS CURIOUS THINGS.   JUST BE STUPID
AND SPEAK PLAIN. AND ITS REVERSE. BE SMART
AND SPEAK NOT.   SAY ONE THING ONCE, THEN
SAY OTHERWISE.
OR ASK WILLIAMS TO TRANSLATE MY OPULENCE . . .
A POEM SHOULD BE A PERFECT TALK. Well, I love
how you talked about love.
YOU COULD SAY EVERY POEM IS A LOVE POEM,
IT JUST DEPENDS ON HOW PERVERSE YOU ARE.
STILL, I CAN ONLY BE SO WRY—THERE IS SUCH A THING
AS TOO MUCH UNDERSTANDING.
A POEM HAS TEASING FINGERS, BUT MY LIFE ENDED
WITHOUT ONE WORD EVER MAKING LOVE TO ME.
TRUTH IS,   I MISS DAVID, AND NOT DYING.

III.

How We Are

The health department worker's
first step into the trailer

disappears
into cockroaches.

A mother and son are living there,
it's Florida, mid-July,

the mother is wearing

a long winter coat, gloves,
a scarf around her face;

she keeps the baby in a thick blanket
to protect him from bites.

There are clouds of roaches flying
in flocks

like birds. Like any of us,
she has no way of explaining her life.

Poem

I was born the same moment as the first moon landing.
I remember watching the fuzzy scene on a small ceiling TV.

My mother's cry a long drawn out *O*—
pure pain and surprise in an Idaho motel room.

Mother's thighs opened wide: I could see the faint skull
of moon, the astronaut emerging from the capsule,
sky a blackness around him, the fluffs of moon-dust
as he toddled about like a man learning to walk.

I heard applause, for everything was possible,
then weeping, the joy of my young father and mother
and the men in the NASA control room—

before them, rows of buttons,
instruments ringing of moonlight,

and there I was for the first time,
bony and bright.

Fertility Woes, So We Go to Breed in Hawaii's Shallow Waters

A humpback emerges like an island, a husband and wife climb atop; each at the extremes of the backbone stands facing the other, he at tail's end, she straddles the blow hole and says, I am standing on a beast that contains more seminal fluid than 10,000 men.

The husband says, let us go down now into our kayaks back to our room and do what it is that mammals do.

Look, says the wife, I am standing on top of a whale near the head, but it's all head, and you are at the tip of the tail, but a whale is all tail.

The man asks the air, where is my daughter? Her hair must be caught somewhere. Something stops her growing from zero.

The whale sings its famous Ave Maria.

Ka-ule-u-Nanahoa or Phallic Rock, a six foot tall stone to sit or sleep on. She sleeps curled up at the top, makes quick smiles as she dreams.

In Hawaiian, sex is called "the floating world." Conception is "clouds and rain." The hammock's belly suspends between two trees. The warm mango moon and magnetism release wave upon wave. Then her thermometer beeps a temporal change. The moon is gendering.

Whales do yoga in the morning to promote fertility; they exhale from their pelvic floor to the roof of their mouths. It's called a *blow*. It makes them more open, less judgmental about suffering a sixteen foot two ton newborn.

O most fertile day; O Pergonal, Danocrine; grunt, click; O ovulation predictor kit.

The Most Beautiful Pigeon in the World

after Russell Edson

A man falls in love with a pigeon. He thinks it's dramatically beautiful, even when it poops. He asks his wife if the pigeon can move in.

The pigeon looks at her sideways with its red Cycloptic eye. The wife says, "I will not have that *eye* in my house!" . . .

He insists the pigeon's beauty sustains him; he even worries the pigeon's dead when it's merely asleep. The pigeon plays coy, leaves a single feather in every room. This affects him. He begins to yearn for a past he never had. He finds himself obsessed with her grey tail feathers, calls her his "little storm cloud." He and the pigeon start a family: small-headed, short-legged, swift-flying. Things go bad. She becomes dull. He feels manipulated as if his pigeon were consciously trying to become the subject of a tragic poem, always pecking, always suspicious, *hhhooo-hoooo-hoo-hoooo.* He stops listening, makes pointed comments about her enormous white rump.

Then one day he fancies an ant. He likes the swing of its hips, not mechanical like other ants, but beautiful, like a good memory he never had . . .

A Worm, a Rat, a Love Poem

(At a poetry reading, a woman asked me if I was the person who wrote the love poem about the worm and the rat. I said no, but felt obligated to try and write it. I now realize the woman may have been insane.)

The worm is both male and female, a fun-loving complex life form with five pairs of hearts. Favorite color: brown. Hobbies include: serious gardening. The rat does his best, though Valentines Day is hard, what with short legs cutting out ten paper hearts.

The worst part for the rat is that worms speak in monologues—in chains of cause and effect. The rat can't mention dinner plans without hearing a long thing about the food chain.

The best part for the worm is not the rat's hairless wormy tail, but his whiskery snout—a worm loves nothing more than to be tickled with rat whiskers up and down. And the rat loves that the worm is naked to the world, a bare probing finger.

The rat is a poet, but still a good husband—unpredictable, which is exciting to a worm. Today a rat with patience, tonight a rat with no expectations, and so on, like one must be when living with such a desirable but temperamental worm.

The beauty of worm is that he/she is utterly vulnerable and good—worms help the world grow. The rat knows that if God is in the form of anything, it's a worm.

The Physics of Ex-Girlfriends

Interactive Physics
   describes the way that matter interacts with other matter,
   i.e., gravity, velocity, compatibility, etc.
   More than the orbit of planets
   or the energy transformations during a game of pool,
   ex-girlfriends
   are a study of underlying forces whose memories penetrate
   the entire universe,
   endowing personal space with measurable physical properties.
   If a heart is dropped from 50 miles off the ground:
   the velocity would be D., who was too nice for me
   and eventually met a nice Swedish boy. One rule of physics is
   objects at rest stay at rest, which is not true when the object is
       lied to:
   L. said the hickies on her neck were burns from her curling iron.
   Physics has a lot of emotion. I was in pain when
   living with J., who was an inclined plane.
   With energy,
   it's just a matter of adding two together and subtracting
   the energy lost to friction: J. had a heart,
   but I slept with M. and then K.;
   disregard has gravity and weight.

Acceleration
   is the rate at which velocity changes.
   B. was a virgin,
   and then not.
   Momentum is an object's resistance
   to changing its current path and speed.
   Momentum can't be lost; it can only be transferred.
   If you have sex with C., she screams her own name—
   the momentum goes through you and into the earth. This will
   change the rotational speed of the earth by a very small amount,
   but the change
   is cancelled out by the opposite force of C.'s light moustache
   and bulky personal baggage.
Things do fall,
   and this never changes on Earth. Especially

when K. ends every sentence with, "What's that supposed to
    mean?"
Yet the common laws
of physics begin to deteriorate on small scales. The way T.
overused the word "amazing," L. licked her lips obsessively,
and M. always made me macaroni and cheese to make up.

Quantum physics
    is the physics of the incredibly small . . .
    it says electrons
    don't orbit like planets, they form blurred clouds of probabilities:
    C. smelled funny, but liked to wear black lingerie.
    Thus, sometimes
    a particle acts like a particle and sometimes acts like a wave.
    A. was sexy, but she believed in Adam and Eve.

Note:
    All equations are uneven.
    The engine of the universe is memory, a substitute for love.
    Dark space is long black hair; stars are lost names and numbers,
    distant addresses.

The Distance in Restaurants

That couple
In silence total

One wall to another
A quiet corner

They read together
And they have been read

Good bad
All been said

They eat nothing
Rare or sweet

"Water"
The waiter said

And went his way to get
The bread

Love & Other Problem Verbs

I   am/was   you
You   are/were   me
We   are/were   forms of *lie* and *lay*

Of Love
Past Perfect:
            I, you, he/she, we, they   had laid, lied, been

She talks and *he doesn't* (not *she talk* and *he don't*).

If I *were* [not *was*] you, I'd proceed more cautiously.

Waiting silently for your prey is a verbal phrase.

begin   began   begun
cling   clung

Who is the subject of *will hurt*, not the object of *know*.

When? Where? What? Why?

At a specific time
    at the edge of something
    at a meeting place
On a day
    on a street
In a year
By a landmark

The red roses were [not *was*] *a wonderful surprise.*
Even when you make a mistake—You smell especially *sweetly*
            this year—

Marriage: Field or Meadow?

He said, "What a lovely field."
      She said, "You mean meadow."
"Well, it's a field."
      "Yes, but a meadow is for grazing or growing."
      She'd heard it from a farmer's wife.
He said that she's probably mistaken, thinking *fallow*.
      She frowns, "A farmer's wife knows what fallow is."
He wants it confirmed by other farmers' wives.
      Then back and forth the rest of their lives.

Marriage

At the end of a pier,

a couple stands
at arms length:
with one hand,
each grips the
throat of the
other and staring
into each other's
eyes catalogues
the reasons why
they should and
would never kill.

In automatic
understanding,
they drop their
hands and shake
hands as if old
friends greeting
in happy surprise,
glad the other
is alive.

They embrace
a quick forgiveness,
then close
whisperings
of who they are.

The lake is calm.
Beneath the sun's
heavy hand,
it receives
the wind's
thousand kisses.

Ode to Julie Christie

At thirteen, sappy with masculinity and totally pathetic,
I would pretend like every boy pretending
to get the girl: I dreamt you came to me needing saving.
When everyone wanted Farrah, I wanted you
in *Heaven Can Wait*.
After school, I fantasized scenes no less
fantastic than Buck Henry as an angel and Warren Beatty
as a millionaire quarterback corpse who gets the girl.
James Mason as Gabriel says,
It's all probability and outcome in heaven.
So, somehow you came to my 8th grade basketball game,
and in the gym that's also my cafeteria,
I make a last-second shot, and the girl with the golden heart
and hair straight from the movie
sees past my skinny legs
and falls
for me.

We talk of where to live outside the world of parents and directors,
a place we could stare at each other forever . . .
maybe it's Greece
dreamed up by Keats, *Forever warm and still to be enjoyed.*
Like the love of which Diotima told Socrates,
our poetry, how it was of its nature neither good nor beautiful,
its desire was the good,
its desire was the beautiful.

In my memory, you lean back again.
You never failed to appear, and I search myself for what was
so briefly,
a boy staring from a bed.
I stroke your hair of sunburnt grasses
and hope to be
your quarterback, or your millionaire.
I reach shyly beneath your English tweed, reach
for breasts floating cold to the touch, for the need to
feel everything at once . . .

Ageless in the right light, in the soft focus of close-ups
you were the absence I felt, the girl that never is.
For a boy there's no confusion,
knowing not through knowledge but a daylight praying—
love is true.

In the end, when Warren Beatty finds you,
 and you pause, reading his eyes, and say,
"Yes, I'd love to have a cup of coffee with you,"
I cried the way we all do,
 beside myself with myself
wanting what I can't touch.

The Rollerway

I should mention Linda Cox. We were thirteen,
and she was more nice than pretty—
extra-large nose, small mouth and chin, and as I said, nice . . .
       the kind of girl you shake hands with
       hello and
goodbye.

At the Rollerway, the "snowball skate"—
boys and girls face each other from a distance,
music unwinds, lights dim, and the lucky and handsome
       picked one by one. . . .
You knew within the length of a song, the hot honesty of puberty.

Then, someone else
held out her hand. There was baby powder in her palm.
She was a pro. We circled. Never spoke.
       A disco ball dressed us in stars—
on polished wood our brightness shot past
the snack bar, racks of shoes and socks—
she skated fast and I held on—the Bee Gees looping like a rosary—
my moving
       circle of girl,
orbiting heart in a soft sweater, tight
Ditto jeans flaring, her electric blue eye shadow and thick mascara,
her bubble gum lip gloss, petite turned-up nose, hair full
and feathered, sparkles on her cheekbones.
       A Friday night's blur and hum of building speed,
and the sight of Linda Cox crying.

       Afterward, heartsick,
I tried to look hard as a man can with braces, waiting for his mom.
And I felt sexy for my lack of sex,
shark tooth necklace,
reckless in my baby hair mustache. That's all I needed then,
       and some gum,
not a job or even a good job, no washer and dryer,
just myself
dressed and waiting. My parents would pay for the rest.

Roofing the Library

for Larry Janowski

The only true carpenter
we called Ziggy, and he played
an old phonograph each day,
all day, Polish jazz for a whole
summer, the same woman and
accordion crying as one.
The heat and weight,
the weight and heat of those heavy
leaves we laid like pages over tar.
I needed money. I wanted
to live to be other than young,
to sleep with the pretty girls
who carried books close to their hearts.
Lunch breaks, I read Salinger
or Vonnegut, ate from sacks
on which my mother wrote
my name. The men would smoke
and speak like music, laugh and argue.
"In Poland," Ziggy said,
"we don't work like this, like rabbits.
We take our time. But we come
to America because in Poland,
everyone is carpenter."
I tried to imagine it, a place
where everyone
measures correctly, builds slowly.
Ziggy said when he came
to this country he knew nothing.
Every day he had to start
at the beginning.

First Sex

I said, Let's get naked. We were bodies
in her parents' bed pretending to be married.
She said, I'm giving you this.

There was no light, no windows;
she wore her body closely; she wanted
it dark, a descent:

I wanted more than anything to see; we
tangled like ghosts, in silence, by degrees, a grim
argument of limbs, no one to save us.

Her coarse nest was a felt interior;
she pulled on my penis, as if that made sense.
There was more and more. Below me,

the bed sounded; the dog snored in the corner.
It was daytime. For a moment, I thought God
had taken the light. Not that I entered her,

but descended: I left her and came back and
left her and came back, a whole lifetime of bad
decisions in quick succession:

my breath became little mated breaths;
and then from the darkness, calm and concerned,
Are you having an asthma attack?

Light returned when she was fully clothed.
I saw that her parents made her into a particular shape.
She asked me to dress in the closet. My body felt estranged

as if I had reached some ultimate end.
The nuns said Jesus said this was a sin.
How difficult even to begin, and then it's over.

New Love Crosses Busy Street

the touchingness of two teens waiting for a storm of cars
how they hold thin arms around thin waists
how in the traffic's gusts they bend like young birches
how blind and deaf to the world coming right then left

their innocent embrace
their feelings single as a stream
their future bright as bleached wood
never looking they step lightly into the street

their legs thin as hairs they stride over the never-stopping strangers
how they float like water-bugs in love amid the city's furious river

Common House-Spider

Spiders hatched in my
        hair. For
a month

I would be
        shaving or
talking or writing and
        one
at a time
        they rapelled
past my

nose. At first
        I was terrified,
they would not wash out,
        but over time
I grew protective,
        unapologetic.
Just babies

        testing
their spinnerets.
        Like new poems, some
would lower only part
        way, then retract.
It's bad luck

        to kill a spider,
especially
        a house-spider.
Reality is
        we all kill—some poison,
some squish with a kleenex,
        others slap
with a magazine or
        overkill with a shoe.

When I see clearly,
        I see we're
all the same:
        show ourselves when
we wish we hadn't.
        On good days I know
nothing lives long.
        I hold my wife
as gently as
        the spiders
I release
        on my front lawn.

        The way we are,
we skitter to where
        home is,
move our arms and legs,
        live
in darkness and in love.

The Sky Over Walgreens

This week I wore the same suit to a wedding and a funeral.
At the funeral, nothing was sung, little was said.
The wedding all poetry and piano. Obviously,
the wedding white, the funeral black. Sunny both days.
>   My suit a mist of gray, at once a version of white with
>   traces of hopeful greens,
but too, threads of fading blue and gold,
the color of cold fear. I didn't know either party well.
The funeral was small, the wedding extravagant.
The wedding a promise the funeral fulfills:
richer, poorer, better, worse, sickness, death.

It's late, the sun setting over Walgreens,
and I feel ridiculous and fortunate with my short shopping list:
a vaporizer,
>   an electric blanket, a Hershey Bar with almonds to help
>   her go on, I need paper to print poems, a softer tooth-
>   brush for my aging gums, and my own bar of chocolate
>   (a reminder that life is sweet and difficult to share).
The sun checks its watch, the sky is thick with clouds, gray with
a wash of rose—neither day's off-white, nor night's closewoven
black.
>   The sky tries to clear its mind, remembers
thunder began the world, life sparked with a lightning strike—
the first amino acid now telephone wires strung between false
trees,
shining cars and bodies, a parking lot in the rain at closing time.

Ode to an Insect in Wet Paint

Small winged life, you stick to what you think you know,
Caught in late spring thinking *meadow*.

You struggle with your tiny might,
You fight the very physics of existence,

Your frantic feelers tell you everything but why.
I too question the rightness of Sage Green. I wait. You dry.

The house needs a new roof, a more solid foundation. I wait.
I wait.

You, smallest of abstract artists
Splashed yourself against a canvas.

Now you know.
Art is death. Life is not a sanctuary. A house is not a flower.

In the Blue Stairwell

("Windows into the Body" exhibit: Chicago Museum of Science and Industry)

They cut him in horizontals—
half-inch sections
with a power saw
from ear to ear and down across his neck, torso, arms, thighs,
      knees, shins,
to his smallest toe
As if you could see through someone from above or below
He is arranged
      like dozens of unframed paintings of steak
His mosaic   a rusted flat yellow heart   grey flap of lung
         its specks of blue tar like squinting stars
     bulb of penis
     wrists like an agate slice you might buy
in the gift shop   hang from a
key chain

She, more whole—four vertical pieces of herself (each a half-inch
thick) from crown down through her pelvis
Her long panels are displayed like four pages opening and spining
out from the wall
You can stand as if inside her,
see her full profile on your right and left
     And like Blake's shapeless souls descending to hell,
      her selves slouch thin but heavy, unforgiven in their bag
         of skin
Her outline, almost human:
her few electric strands of pubic hair   the amber impression of a
        nipple   her breast's receding beach   the peek at a
small piece of lip   a small breathless nostril   her last loyal eyelash
        a bit of ear

Inside, her parts are arrowed with words, her heart is labeled
      heart, her ribs marked *true* and *false*

This Woman looks blind and sideways at herself;
This Man, like a deck of cards unshuffled, looks up and down for
      what he was

Our heavy creative brain floats in a pool, its waves stimulate the
whole enormous Tongue, our throat's muscular yet sensitive heart,
which leads Blake to say,

As a man is, so he sees
From the subterraneous Mouth and precarious Teeth, the earth is
declared a perfect Eye or the eye a perfect Earth, from its aqueous
ocean to its lit pupil, it can detect a lighted candle 1 mile away, can
see up to   10,000 colors

The Heart, like us, beats its fist but works only as much as it has to:
in an average life   between beats   it rests for 40 years

Between the lost and found and the coat check, near the restrooms
and the public phone, between the Main Floor and the Balcony, near
the baby chick hatchery, the fairy castle,
      Petrochemicals, Polymers and You,
past the kids petting plastic cows, behind How to Ship Spent
Nuclear Fuel,
before you Enter the Internet, below Virtual Embryo,

not the sold-out Titanic exhibit, not an actual locomotive, not the
line for the flight simulator, nor the combine ride
The sign says, *Basic Science: The Head, The Heart*

Not on the map of Special Exhibits, two bodies in pieces in the Blue
Stairwell on the landing between
      the coal mine and the Nazi submarine
Anonymous as anyone, this man, this woman died in 1940,
were frozen, then sliced

This Is That Sonnet

after Carlos Drummond De Andrade

the dirty the daisies the blurt the bloom
the diddle the titter the tussle the tenderness
the jollity the recoil the go-between the groom
the festive the fright the quintessence the dress
the time the thereby the unchaste the cake
the start the love-arc the swoon the uproot
the bumptious the jangle the jostle the ache
the whoopee the buttery the fruit the *billets-doux*
the ticklish the picnic the blushing the oh
the flirty the wordy the gaga the hay
the kiddies the agony the snow the outgrow
the goo-goo the smooch the fix the fray
the wan the grandma the migraine the mown
the syrupy the daughterly the bone of my bones

The Way We Sleep

A faint wind sound mixed with snow brushes our house and
you're sleeping like you always sleep—flying through a dream—
on your stomach, legs straight and to-
>   gether,
one foot cupped in the other, left arm tight to your side, the right
in a fist above your head fighting the wind, and you're looking off
your side of the bed into the abyss of your inner
>   eyelids
where you see what keeps you talking and laughing in your sleep.
Jealous, I woke you once to know if I was there: you said,
All I can tell you is, it involved the Queen of Eng-
>   *land,*
giving someone a facial, and the Red Baron. In bed there's nowhere to
go but to know we are separate. You let yourself forget, breathe
easily, sleep weightless and brave.

I feel fallen, strangely awake. I curl in on myself, burrow like
a fox caught in heavy
>   snow,
I lie on my side faced away from my life waiting for its storm.

Old Ladies in the Universe

All that can be
in every old lady's gaping mouth—the O of time, the egg
                                        of birth, the cave of death.
To the circle of old ladies silent in the dining hall,
in this white room white

                                        as a nursery,
the nurse loudly as to children, "Eat! Eat! Drink your milk!"
The whole eternal

                        universe in how—
unmoving and soundless—the women stare out as from a distance,
eyes spinning
                inward,
a cataract whirl of personal cosmic dust. And though they are
forced to eat
            and do not think to wipe their chins,
their pure white hair uncombed rises like fires—

                                        great dying stars

they were once young mothers. . . .

In their vacillating senses,
the mind, the elements, time and nature and action collapse,
                                coalesce,
the gravity and pressure in their plates
complete
            with broccoli, peanut butter and jelly sandwiches cut small,
            vitamin-fortified pudding, macaroni and cheese.

                                My grandmother
(who has eaten everything) turns to me, her eyes teary with pleasure,
and says,
            "You can't imagine how great it is."
She repeats this—as I put the straw to
                                her lips.

About the Author

Chris Green's poems have appeared in numerous publications, including *Poetry, Verse, Black Clock, North American Review, RATTLE, 5 AM, Poet Lore,* and *Poetry East.* He lives in Evanston, Illinois, where he teaches writing at Loyola University and DePaul University. He is also a Visiting Fellow at the DePaul University Humanities Center.

Other recent titles from Mayapple Press:

Mariela Griffor, *HOUSE*, 2007
    Paper, 50 pp, $14.95 plus s&h
    ISBN 978-0932412-539
John Repp, *Fever,* 2007
    Paper, 36 pp, $11.95 plus s&h
    ISBN 978-0932412-522
Kathryn Kirkpatrick, *Out of the Garden*, 2007
    Paper, 80 pp, $14.95 plus s&h
    ISBN 978-0932412-515
Gerry LaFemina, *The Book of Clown Baby/Figures from the Big Time Circus Book,* 2007
    Paper, 60 pp, $14.95 plus s&h
    ISBN 978-0932412-508
Nancy Botkin, *Parts That Were Once Whole*, 2007
    Paper, 72 pp, $14.95 plus s&h
    ISBN 978-0932412-492
David Lunde, *Instead,* 2007
    Paper, 72 pp, $14.95 plus s&h
    ISBN 978-0932412-485
Zilka Joseph, *Lands I Live In*, 2007
    Paper, 42 pp, $12.95 plus s&h
    ISBN 978-0932412-478
Johanny Vásquez Paz, *Poemas Callejeros/Streetwise Poems*, 2007
    Paper, 74 pp, $14.95 plus s&h
    ISBN 978-0932412-461
Larry Levy, *I Would Stay Forever If I Could and New Poems,* 2007
    Paper, 60 pp, $12.95 plus s&h
    ISBN 0-932412-45-9
Christine Hamm, *The Transparent Dinner*, 2006
    Paper, 90 pp, $15.95 plus s&h
    ISBN 0-932412-44-0
Kathleen Tyler, *The Secret Box*, 2006
    Paper, 74 pp, $14.95 plus s&h
    ISBN 0-932412-43-2
Rachel Eshed, *Little Promises*, 2006 (bilingual Hebrew/English)
    Paper, 104 pp, $16 plus s&h
    ISBN 0-932412-42-4

For a complete catalog of Mayapple Press publications, please visit our website at *www.mayapplepress.com.* Books can be ordered direct from our website with secure on-line payment using PayPal, or by mail (check or money order). Or order through your local bookseller.